How To...
PLAY ROCK LEAD GUITAR

BY BROOKE ST. JAMES
TRANSCRIBED & EDITED BY TROY NELSON

To access video visit:
www.halleonard.com/mylibrary

Enter Code
7990-4825-5144-2151

ISBN 978-1-4950-2325-5

HAL•LEONARD®
CORPORATION
7777 W. BLUEMOUND RD. P.O. BOX 13819 MILWAUKEE, WI 53213

In Australia Contact:
Hal Leonard Australia Pty. Ltd.
4 Lentara Court
Cheltenham, Victoria, 3192 Australia
Email: ausadmin@halleonard.com.au

Visit Hal Leonard Online at
www.halleonard.com

CONTENTS

ABOUT THE AUTHOR

Brooke St. James got his start on guitar at age 9. His obsession with an old acoustic guitar sitting in the corner at his grandmother's house paid off when he was finally allowed to take the guitar home. A self-taught musician, Brooke spent endless hours listening to records and began to play along with the likes of Kiss, Aerosmith, Ted Nugent, Queen, Cheap Trick, Journey, and more. He joined his first band at the age of 16 playing with older musicians in night clubs. "It was a lot easier to be in bars underage back then!" After graduating high school, Brooke ventured out with a Florida-based rock act who toured the West Coast for a year straight, thus getting schooled in the ways of the road at age 17.

"From that point, I played with a few regional cover bands that really helped broaden my playing. It was funk, rock, blues, pop, reggae, you name it."

In the mid-'80s, Brooke relocated to Milwaukee where he joined forces with Moxy Roxx. Moxy was filling large venues, which garnered the attention of Cheap Trick manager Ken Adamany. Moxy released one studio album, *Victims of the Night*, which grew to cult status and grabbed the attention of a few major labels. Unfortunately, a half-hearted effort by management killed any potential for a deal and major-label interest soon fizzled.

After struggling for five years with Moxy, Brooke felt that if anything was going to happen, he would need to get to Los Angeles or New York City. After some contacts were made, it was off to New York to form what would become Tyketto, a hard rock group that was eventually signed to Geffen Records. Brooke wrote and recorded four studio albums and did numerous world tours before leaving the band officially in 2014.

Brooke did a three-year stint in Las Vegas with classic rock act Yellow Brick Road. As of 2016, Brooke is currently playing with the bands Rhythm Method, Light Up (A Tribute to Styx), and the Yuletide Conspiracy Project, as well as doing session work and writing songs for a forthcoming solo album.

INTRODUCTION

Hello, my name is Brooke St. James. In this book/video, I'm going to take you through some fundamentals of playing good, solid rock lead guitar. I'm an ear-trained player, so we won't get into a bunch of theory; we'll just stick to the basics, with a little flash thrown in. Alright, let's get started...

ABOUT THE VIDEO

Each chapter in the book includes a full video lesson, so you can see and hear the material being taught. To access all of the videos that accompany this book, simply go to **www.halleonard.com/mylibrary** and enter the code found on page 1. The music examples that include video are marked with an icon throughout the book, and the timecode listed with each icon tells you exactly where on the video the example is performed.

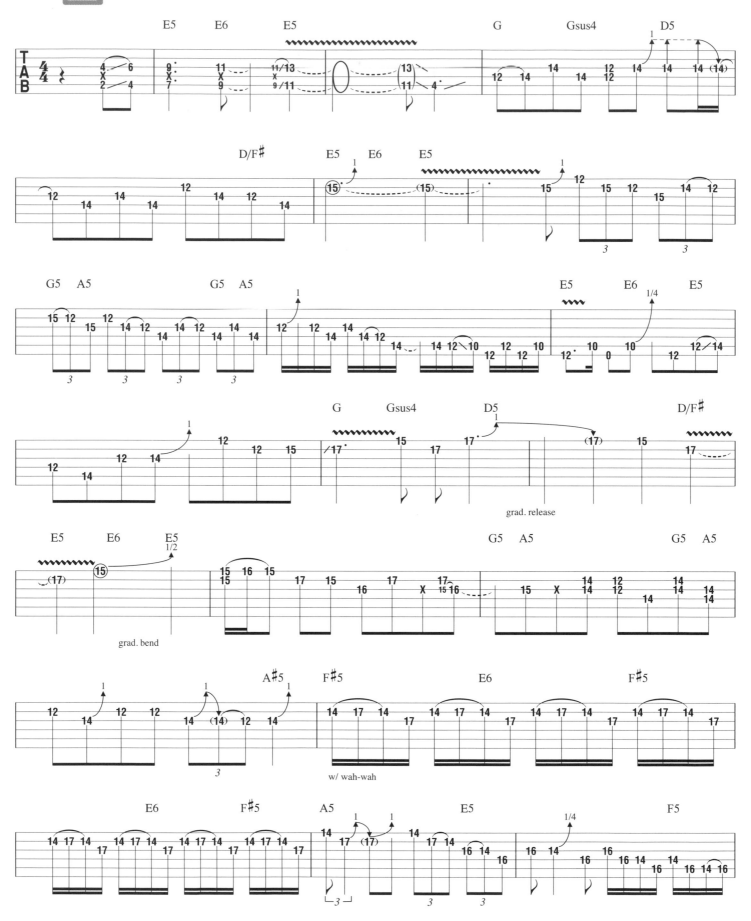

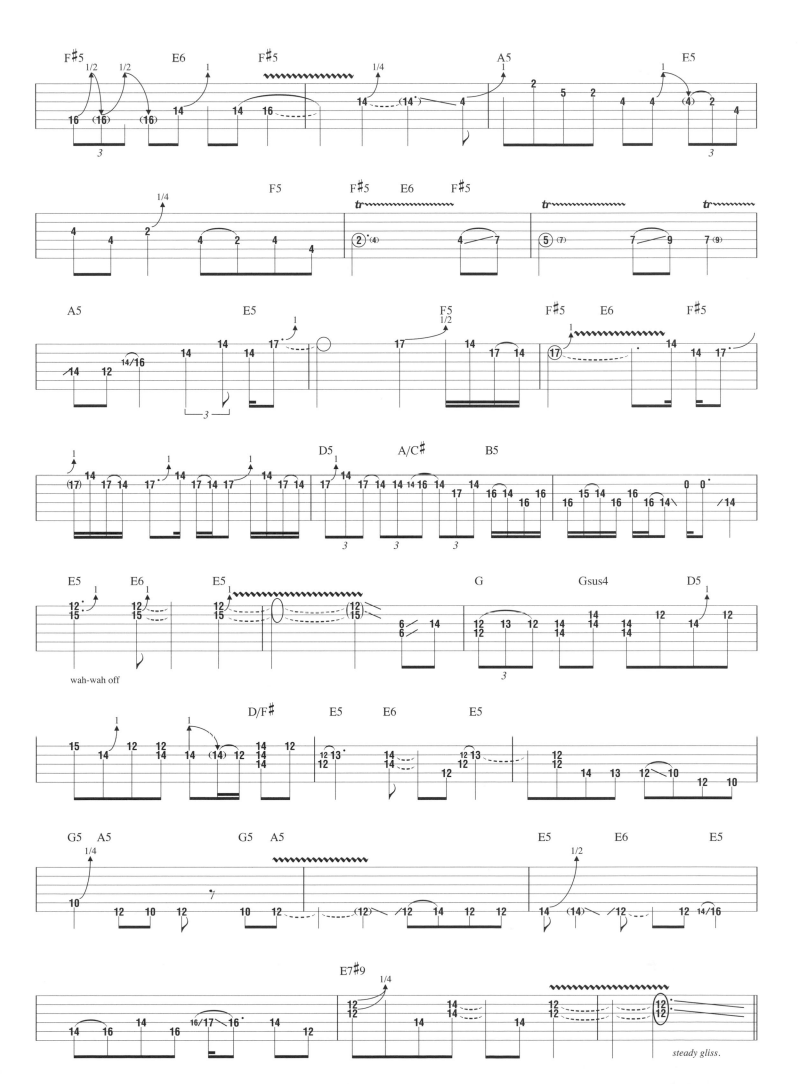

CHAPTER 1
PICKING

GUITAR PICKS

The first thing I want to talk about is the guitar pick. I use a medium-to-heavy gauge (.88 mm), standard-shaped pick. As a rule of thumb, the lighter the pick, the less attack you're going to have. Acoustic players who do a lot of strumming and want a nice, even attack use lighter picks. The more aggressive you want to get, the heavier your pick should be. I'm somewhere in between the two.

I can get pretty aggressive with my medium-gauge picks. I like medium-gauge picks because heavy picks are less forgiving. Medium picks give you some flexibility—literally! You need to find one that works for you. If you start somewhere in the middle, you'll find the gauge that suits you best.

FLATPICKING

You're going to be *flatpicking* all the time when playing lead guitar. Flatpicking involves dragging the pick across the strings.

For rhythm guitar, I tend to loosen my grip a bit so that there's a little more pick on the strings, but when I play lead guitar, I tend to expose a little less of the pick, which allows me to control the pick as it crosses the strings. At times, I'll even use the side of my thumb to hit the string.

As you start to experiment with flatpicking, you'll want to use a good exercise that focuses on one note, like this:

 PICKING 1 - 1:52

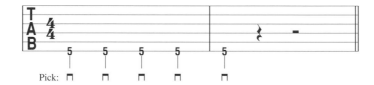

As you can hear, every time I hit the string, the note sounds slightly different than the time before. I'm playing the same note, but I'm striking the string at different angles and at different places up and down the string. This is a big part of your identity as a guitar player: finding the spot that sounds good to your ears.

Some guys play way back by the bridge, which is reminiscent of Jimmy Page:

 PICKING 2 - 2:28

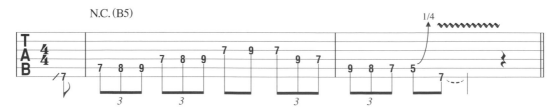

Playing near the bridge gives you a much brighter, brasher attack:

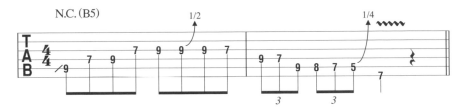

If you move forward, towards the neck, you still get a good attack but the tone is much "rounder" and warmer.

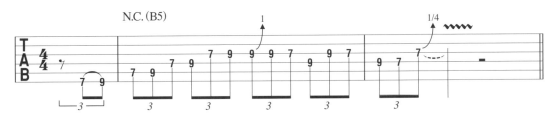

DOUBLE PICKING

Next, I want to discuss *double picking*, or *alternate picking*. Double picking is really no different than the upstrums and downstrums of rhythm guitar playing.

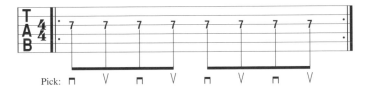

In the example above, I moved between downstrokes and upstrokes. Be patient—you won't develop this technique overnight. But it's very important that, after you determine which way you like to hold the pick, you start to develop your alternate picking.

The guitar pick is also a pretty effective "weapon" for other things. You can get all kinds of neat sounds out of it. Pick slides, scrapes, and burns are great for starting songs or transitioning into a new song section. You can't go wrong with 'em! To play lead guitar, you need a pick and you need to learn how to use it!

CHAPTER 2

PENTATONIC SCALES

MINOR PENTATONIC

In this chapter, I want to talk to you about the *minor pentatonic* scale. Learning this scale for the first time is like an epiphany—the sky opens up. And once you learn it, you'll never forget it. A guy showed me the scale when I was really young and I was like, "I get it now!" It's a way to connect the dots when you're playing blues-rock guitar.

Minor pentatonic is a relatively simple scale, with five different positions. I want to share with you the first of those positions, which is the mainstay of blues-rock playing. We're going to play it in the key of E minor, starting with your index finger on the 12th fret and your ring finger on the 15th fret of the high E string.

 PENTATONIC 1 - 0:58

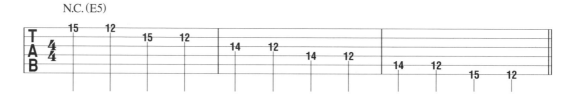

It's a relatively simple pattern to grasp, and you can ascend the scale, too:

 PENTATONIC 2 - 1:25

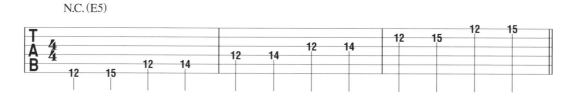

MAJOR PENTATONIC

The E *major pentatonic* is easy to nail down because it's the exact same shape, played three frets lower:

 **PENTATONIC 3 - 2:15**

You can really hear the difference in the tonality of those two scales.

PASSING TONES

Now we're going to talk about something really cool—*passing tones*. Check this out:

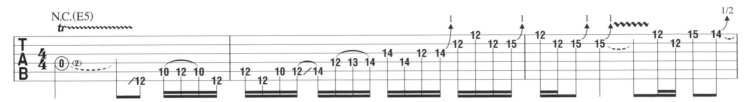

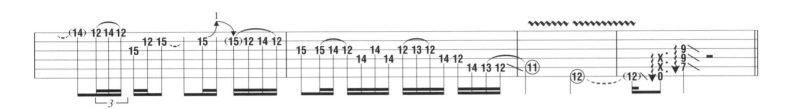

In the example above, I interjected passing tones into the minor pentatonic scale. I reside mostly in the pentatonic world because I love the blues-rock stuff. As long as I've been playing, I've constantly found new ways to use passing tones. I'm going to show you what they are and then you can interject them any way you want—there really are no rules. You'll find out quickly which ones work and in which ways. Some sound pleasant when you land on them, while others are not so pleasant, depending on what you're playing over. Also, when playing the pentatonic scale in rock 'n' roll, you're going to be moving between major and minor. In the example that I just played for you, I was doing that very thing, and we'll get into that a little later in the book.

Let's take the minor pentatonic scale that you already know and add a few notes to make it sound bluesy:

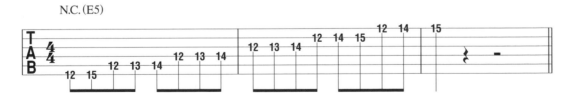

Some of these notes are subject to what you're playing over, especially on the B and high E strings, but most of them can be used in quick passages and they'll sound great:

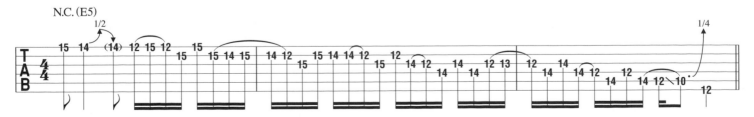

You'll notice that, in these fast passages, I'm not really landing on any of the passing tones. Nevertheless, they are really effective and give some attitude to your lead lines. You'll want to experiment with these passing tones and find out which ones work well for you.

When moving through major and minor pentatonics, you're going to have moments that sound minor, but also incorporate major notes:

 **PENTATONIC 7 - 5:15**

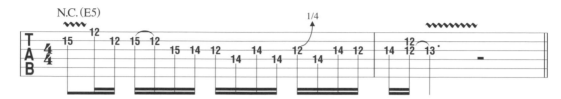

That mixture of major and minor is what gives your lines a really authentic blues vibe:

 **PENTATONIC 8 - 5:25**

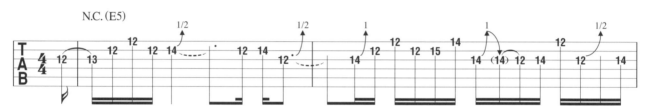

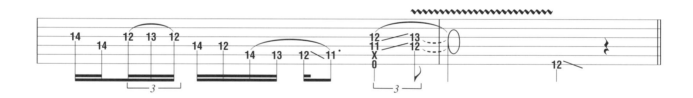

PENTATONIC EXERCISE

Next, I want to show you a little exercise that will help you get acclimated to the minor pentatonic scale. It's one of the first exercises that I learned. Basically, it descends the scale in a pattern of threes.

 **PENTATONIC 9 - 6:01**

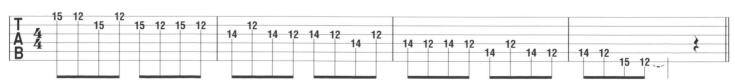

Finally, here's an example that puts together everything we've learned in this chapter:

PENTATONIC 10 - 6:17

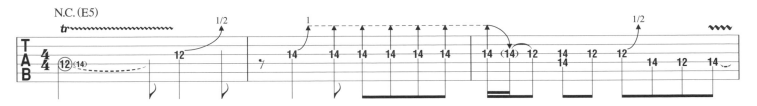

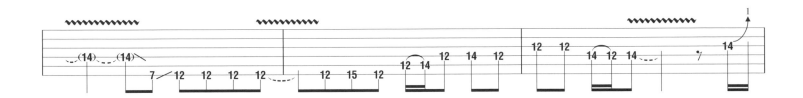

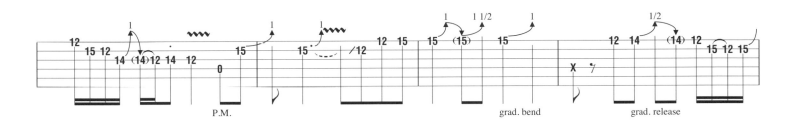

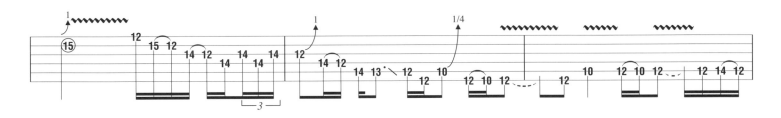

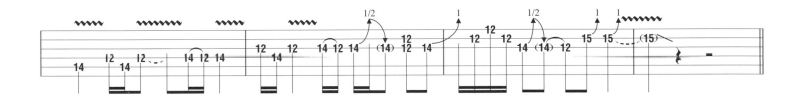

CHAPTER 3
MUTING

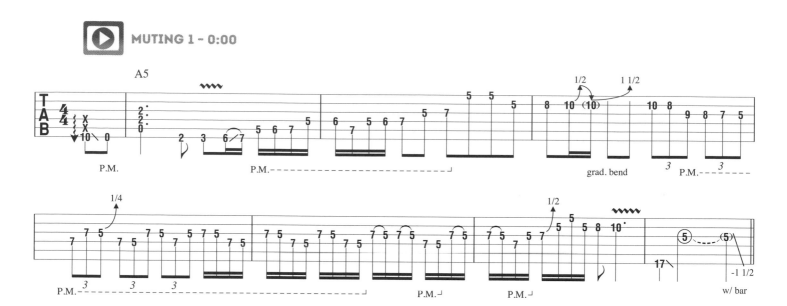

▶ MUTING 1 - 0:00

PALM MUTING

In this chapter, I want to talk to you about *muting*. Lead guitar muting is very similar to the techniques used in rhythm playing. You're still using your right and left hands, but in slightly different ways; you tend to pick your hands up and put them down a little more frequently. Here's a palm-muting example using a pentatonic-type lick:

▶ MUTING 2 - 0:40

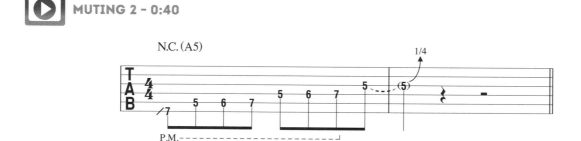

There are a couple of things going on in that example. First, as I play each note, I'm bouncing my hand a little bit to allow the note to come through, but then shutting it down in time for the next one, kind of like a noise gate. I want to let the note through but then calm it down; otherwise, you've got notes bleeding together, which sounds a little lackluster.

Each time I hit a note, my hand is coming down, and every time I bring the pick back up, my hand is doing the same.

▶ MUTING 3 - 1:31

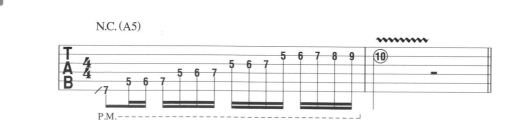

FRET-HAND MUTING

We'll also use our fret hand to mute. There are certain passages that require more fret-hand muting than others. For instance, here's a pentatonic example:

MUTING 4 - 1:48

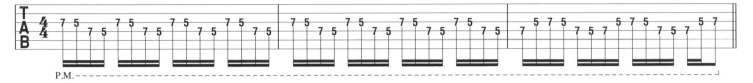

I'm using right-hand palm muting but also bouncing my fret-hand fingers a little to help create the rhythm. As you can see, when I'm getting into the fast pattern, my left-hand index finger is actually coming off the string. Bringing it back in contact with the string helps create the muted rhythm.

Here's another example:

MUTING 5 - 2:27

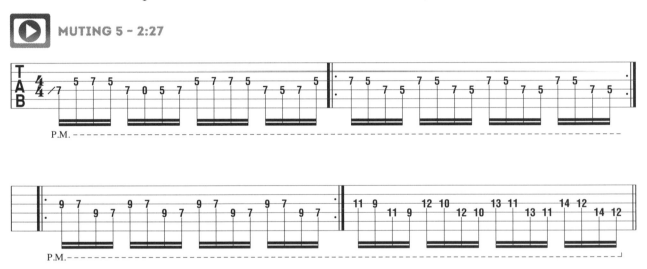

The fret hand, in conjunction with palm muting, is helping to create the muted rhythm that you're hearing.

MUTING EXERCISES

MUTING 6 - 2:41

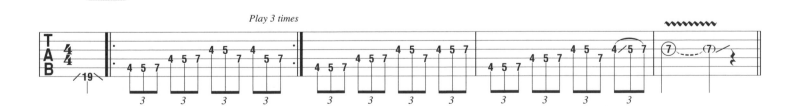

Next, we'll look at a couple of additional things I like to do with my muting, above and beyond the simple pentatonic-based stuff. When playing faster passages, muting is great for creating separation between the notes.

The previous example featured triplets, and it's great for working on your muting. Here's a similar idea broken down into an exercise:

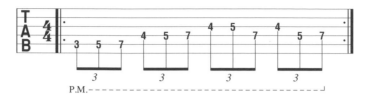

Notice the crisscross pattern on beats 3 and 4. As in the previous example, while I'm picking the notes, I'm lifting my fret hand to let the notes ring out just enough, but not so much that they'll result in a blur.

The following example demonstrates both muted and unmuted notes. You can really tell the difference.

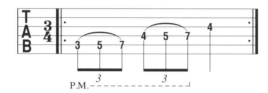

The unmuted notes are more "fluid," but if you want separation, you must incorporate right- and left-hand muting. The left hand is "pulse muting"—it's bouncing and dancing across the strings.

Here's an example that demonstrates left- and right-hand muting in a number of different rhythmic and technical applications:

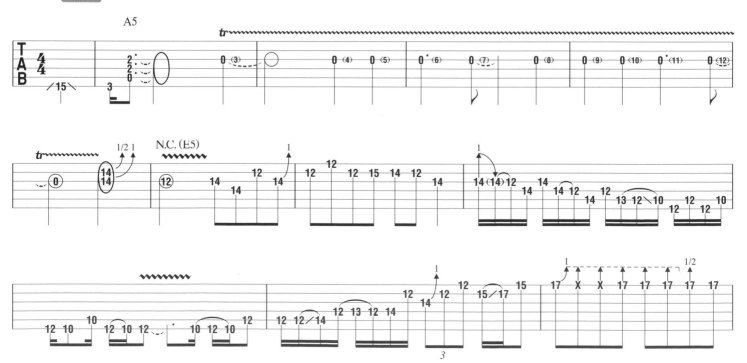

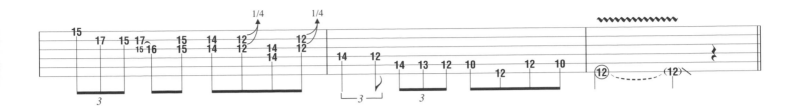

You can introduce muting to almost anything you play—fast triplets, bluesy pentatonic phrases, hammer-ons, pull-offs, etc. Muting is a great dynamic tool, even if you're playing something blazing, like this:

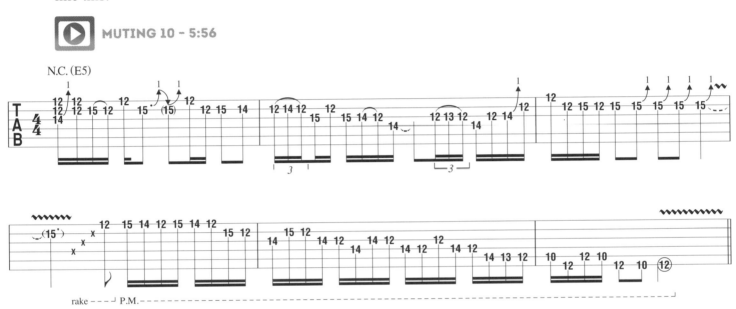

The notes are there and they're ringing, but they're muted. Here's another example:

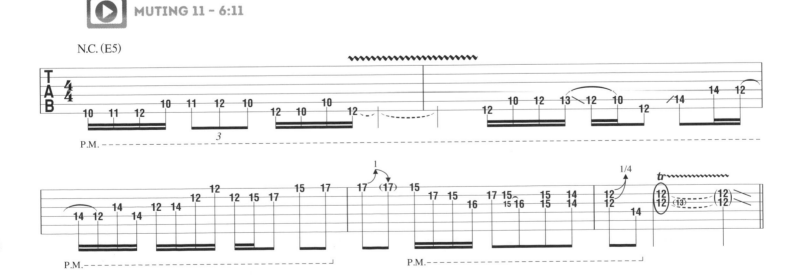

Give it a shot!

CHAPTER 4
VIBRATO

 **VIBRATO 1 - 0:00**

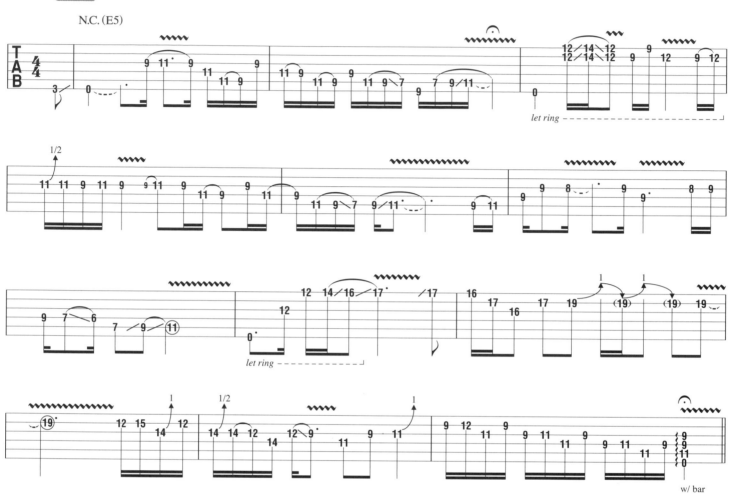

FRET-HAND VIBRATO

Let's talk a little *vibrato* and the techniques you'll want to use to get yours nice and smooth. Start with your ring finger on the G string. Grab the string and just rock it a bit:

 **VIBRATO 2 - 0:58**

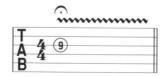

You may notice that I'm not really bending the string up—although that certainly works. To get a smoother, even vibrato, I think it's better to pull south—in other words, towards the bottom of the neck. I'm using my wrist to rock the string, more so than my hand. It's a twisting motion and it can be done slowly or quickly. When I'm doing the faster vibrato, I'm not only rocking my wrist, but I'm pulling my fingers down and together, like a pumping motion.

When you're using vibrato, it's very important to stay in tune. If you're playing over an E chord, you don't want this:

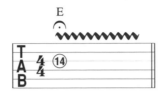

Unless it's for dramatic effect, you want to be in tune. There's going to be some motion in the note because it's modulating, but you want it to maintain a tonal center:

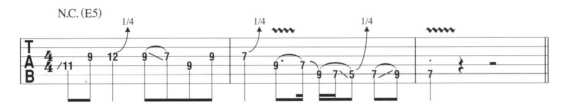

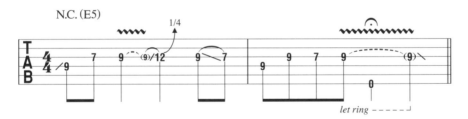

TREMOLO-BAR VIBRATO

If you're using a traditional tremolo bar, aim for the same sort of effect:

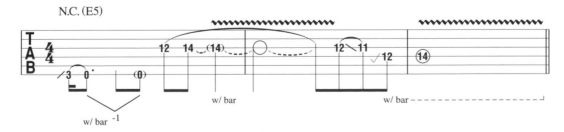

If you're looking for a natural effect, the previous example demonstrates what you want. There's a downward and an upward motion involved. Here's another example:

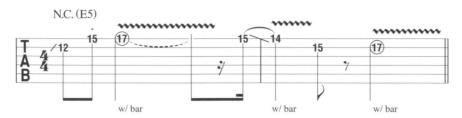

When you use your fingers, you're not just bending up—it's both up and down. The vibratoed note is floating back and forth but it has a tonal center. It's a really wavy, beautiful sound:

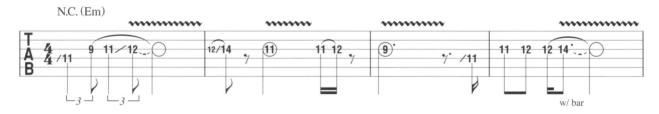

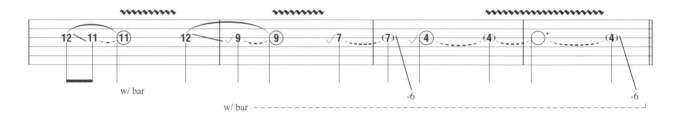

FINGER-SLIDE VIBRATO

I want to show you a vibrato technique that I picked up from guys like George Lynch, Warren DeMartini, and a few other cats.

Instead of shaking a note like this…   …they're doing this:

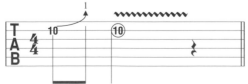   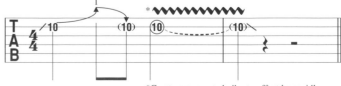

*Create exaggerated vibrato effect by rapidly
sliding fret-hand finger up and down fingerboard,
both above and below target note.

Sometimes you'll see finger-slide vibrato used at the end of a phrase, and other times it will be in the middle of a solo. It will go by quickly, but it's really cool and adds a ferocious sound:

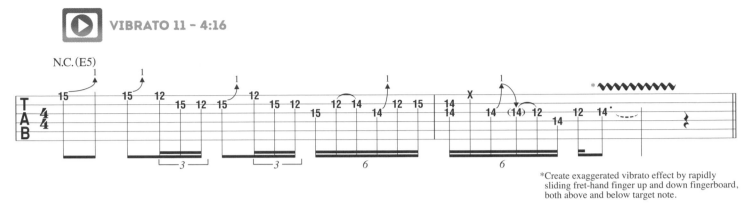

VIBRATO 11 - 4:16

*Create exaggerated vibrato effect by rapidly sliding fret-hand finger up and down fingerboard, both above and below target note.

Finger-slide vibrato is a cool effect that can be used aggressively, but also gently. Experiment with it on your own.

CHORDAL VIBRATO

Now let's look at *chordal* vibrato:

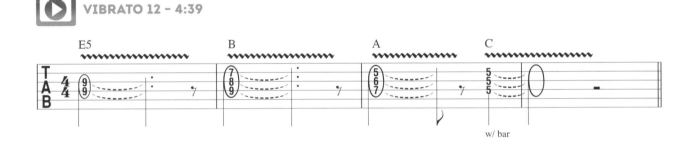

VIBRATO 12 - 4:39

This technique sounds similar to the tremolo bar, which is really what the tremolo bar was designed for:

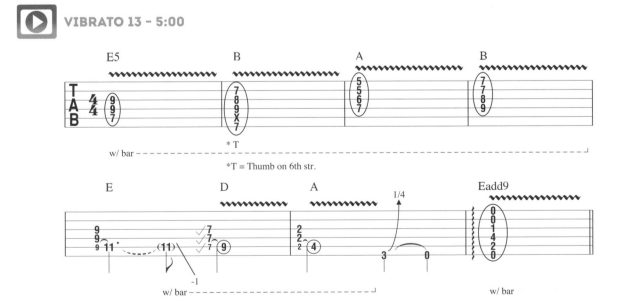

VIBRATO 13 - 5:00

This is a David Gilmour approach to vibrato, which I love.

CHAPTER 5
BENDING

BENDING 1 - 0:00

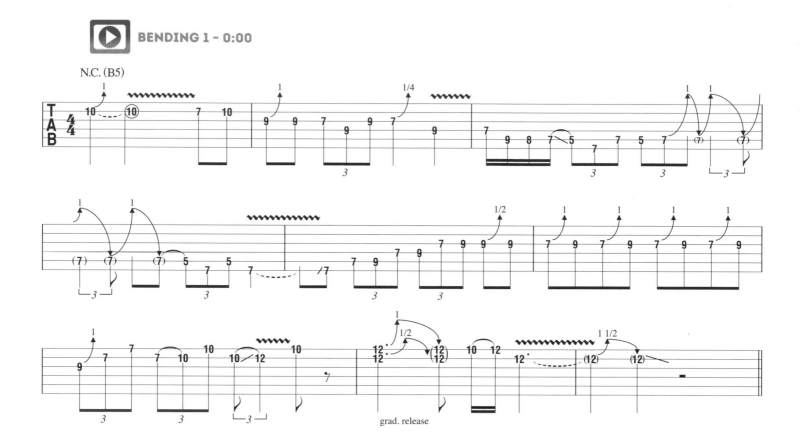

In this chapter, I want to talk about *bending*, a really important technique to lead playing. It's where emotion starts to enter your sound, and I think it's the key to personal expression.

EMOTION OF BENDING

There are so many ways to approach your scales and melodic playing, but unless you introduce some bending, they're going to lack the feeling you need to play in rock 'n' roll bands.

BENDING 2 - 0:52

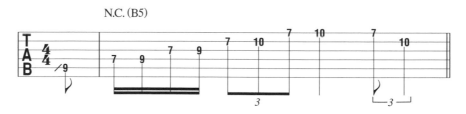

In the example above, you're using the B minor pentatonic scale, and everything sounds great, but it seems to be missing something.

If you put a little wiggle in there…

 BENDING 3 - 1:05

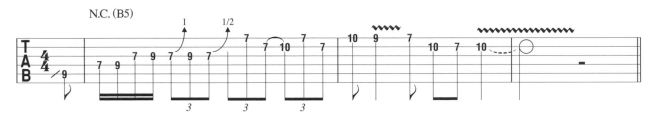

…right away, you start to feel something.

BENDING TO PITCH

Following is an example of something called *bending to pitch*:

 BENDING 4 - 1:17

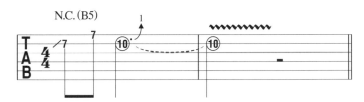

What's going on there is you're looking for a note. Let's say you're playing in the key of B and the first note of your lead is the root note and you want to bend to it. It's very important that you get there. Often, you'll hear out-of-tune bends played by younger guitarists, or guys who aren't as experienced with bending, because they're unable to hear that the bent note isn't quite to pitch. So it's very important that you practice getting to that note.

Unison bends are one way to practice this:

 BENDING 5 - 2:00

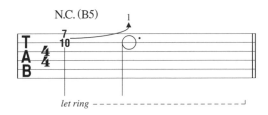

By holding the target note and bending the second string to that pitch, you get familiar with exactly how far you have to go. After you've been doing this awhile, you're just going to start to feel it, as well as hear it. You're going to know how far you need to go to reach that note.

OVER-BENDING

Next, I want to show you something I like to call *over-bending*. I *love* guitar players that do this. Gary Moore and Free's Paul Kossoff did this. It's basically taking what I showed you earlier—that is, bending to pitch—and accentuating the bend, or over-bending.

 BENDING 6 - 3:03

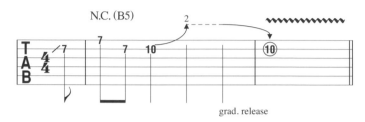

Once again, it's just a matter of bending up to the note you're targeting and then going beyond it. There's a deliberate pitch involved, but once you get beyond the target note, you're just going for the emotion of it. David Gilmour is the master of over-bending.

 BENDING 7 - 3:37

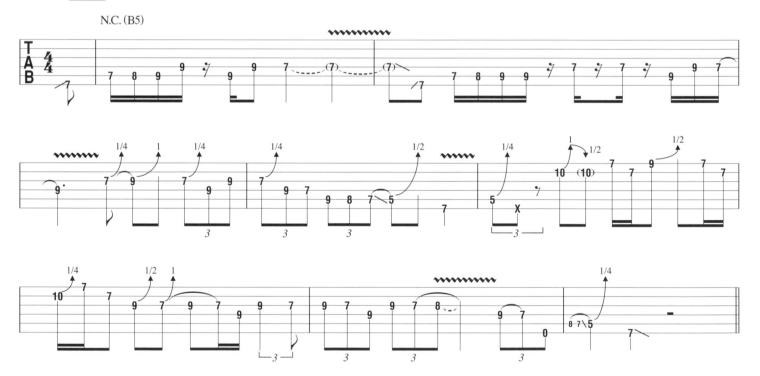

BENDING NORTH AND SOUTH

I call this exercise "bending north and south." It's a matter of becoming more aware of which way you're bending the string. The reason this is important is because there's only so much fretboard to work with, and if you bend in the wrong direction, you're going to bend right off the frets. I use a combination of the two. Again, there's no real rule to it; it's just a common-sense physics thing that you'll start to figure out for yourself.

We're going to start with the D and G strings, which are central to the fretboard. Those are the two strings you may find yourself bending north *and* south the most. Here's an example:

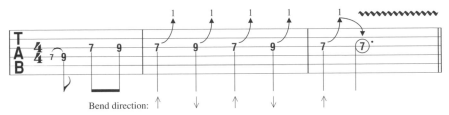

I'm sort of twisting the string, one finger against the other.

Here's a really cool Jeff Beck-inspired lick:

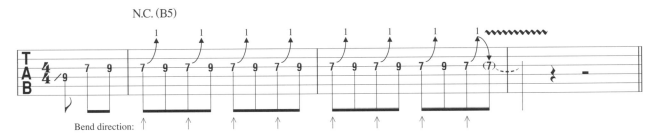

Below is another example in which I'm using both directions:

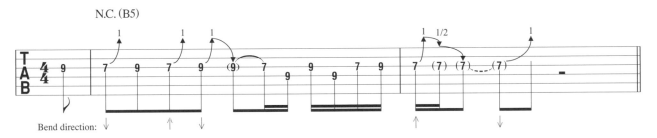

Again, you're using two fingers to bend, but you're twisting in two different directions. Here's another example:

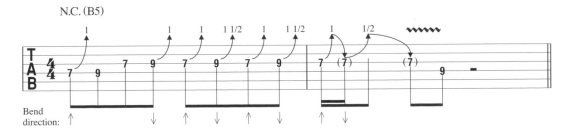

Depending on where you're playing on the fretboard, you may find yourself bending the lower strings more south than north:

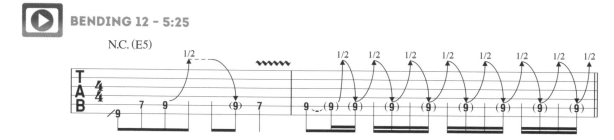

The opposite applies to the higher strings, for bends and vibrato:

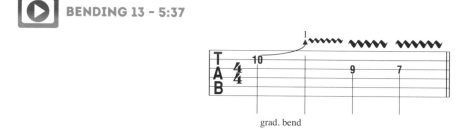

I generally bend south on the lower and middle strings because it's easier to get control of the string.

BENDING AND VIBRATO

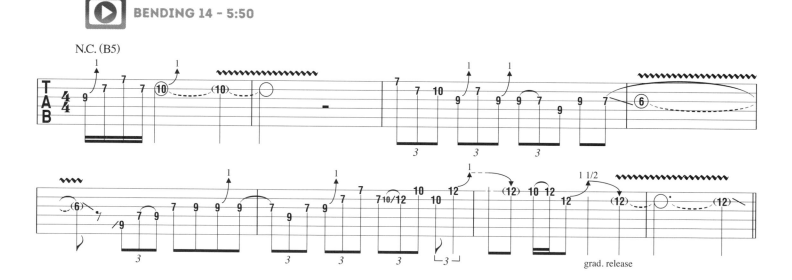

In the previous example, I combined bending and vibrato. Here's another shorter example that also uses both techniques:

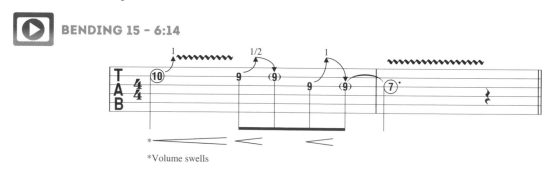

It's very important to interject those two techniques together. Here's another example:

BENDING 16 - 6:21

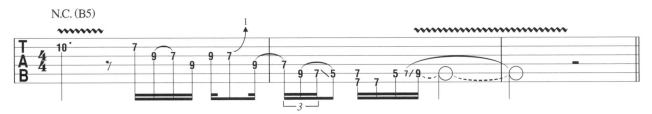

The vibrato is going to give you all the soul, feel, and emotion—as will the bending—but when you put them together, they're even more effective.

BENDING 17 - 6:38

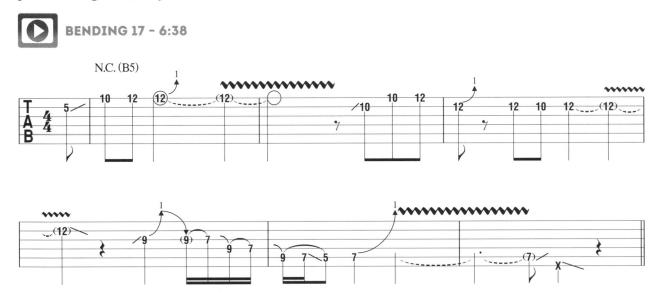

So work on bending with vibrato and try to incorporate this technique into your playing.

DOUBLE-STRING BENDS

Next is a cool lick that I use a lot. I think it was originally something Jimi Hendrix developed, but I learned it while jammin' along to Gary Moore.

BENDING 18 - 6:53

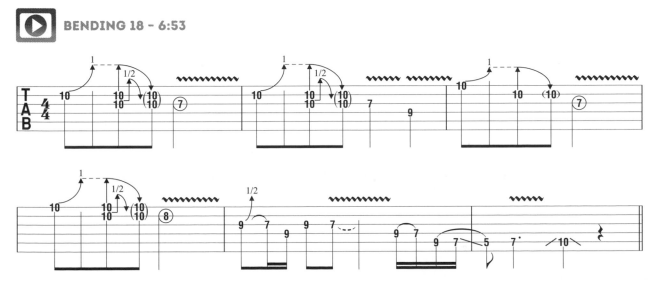

I'm a big Gary Moore fan, and he would grab and bend the B string but come down on the G string by catching it with the same finger:

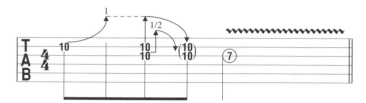

As you bend up on the B string, you catch the G string with the same fret-hand finger, then pick the G string and release both bends. You can do it a couple of ways: 1) you can kill the first note when you get to the top…

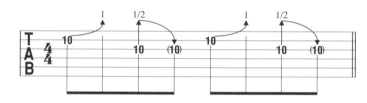

…or 2) you can let them ring together, like in the first example.

It's easy to do on the E and B strings, as well:

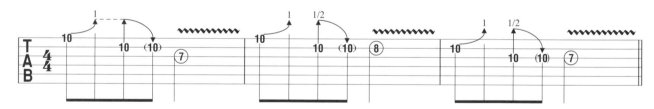

It's a really cool lick, and you might want to incorporate it into your lead playing, too.

CHAPTER 6
ARTICULATIONS

 ARTICULATIONS 1 - 0:00

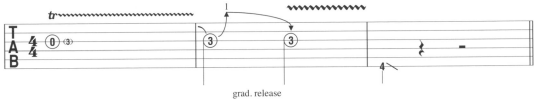

grad. release

In this chapter, we'll cover *hammer-ons* and *pull-offs*, essential parts of playing rock 'n' roll. Guitarists use them in scales, lead runs, and in all kinds of musical situations. I'm going to break them down and show you the basics, then build things up as we go.

HAMMER-ONS

Let's start with an example on the G string using your index finger. Basically, we're just hammering from the open G string to the third fret.

Your fret-hand finger should "hammer" down onto the third fret, causing the note to sound without actually picking it:

 **ARTICULATIONS 2 - 0:43**

It's pretty simple, but there's a real art to it and it's something you'll want to work on slowly, speeding it up as you go.

Next, we'll venture into some two-finger stuff, adding our ring finger one step (two frets) up:

 **ARTICULATIONS 3 - 1:04**

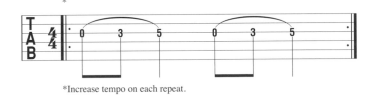

*Increase tempo on each repeat.

As you can see, it's a cool effect. From there, we can get really adventurous and add a third finger:

ARTICULATIONS 4 - 1:27

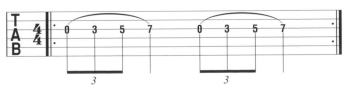

*Increase tempo on each repeat.

PULL-OFFS

The opposite of a hammer-on is a pull-off. In the example below, we will pull off to an open string, starting with the top (highest) note of the previous three-finger pattern. As you lift your finger off of fret 3, pull the string downward slightly so it allows the open string to ring out without picking it again:

ARTICULATIONS 5 - 1:46

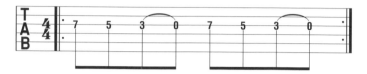

And here's a two-finger pattern:

ARTICULATIONS 6 - 1:56

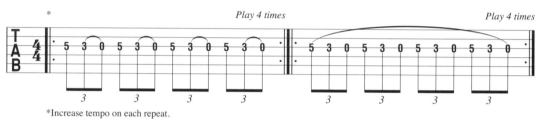

Once you get this down smooth, you won't even need a pick! Your fingers will be pulling the strings by themselves.

Next we have a one-finger trill. You'll learn more about trills in the next section.

ARTICULATIONS 7 - 2:15

Speed will come over time, so don't try to rush it. It's more important that you play the notes cleanly. Another concept to consider is this: when you're grabbing the string, you're almost bending it. You need to get your finger behind the string so that when you pull it and it snaps free, you're sounding another note. You want the volume between the open string and hammered note to be the same, like this:

ARTICULATIONS 8 - 2:52

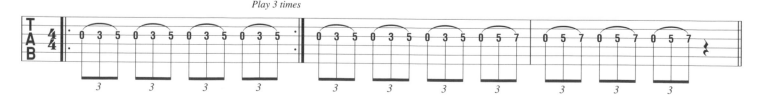

TRILLS

When hammer-ons and pull-offs are played as rapid one- or two-finger combinations, they become *trills*. Here is a trill with an open string and a trill with two fretted notes:

 ARTICULATIONS 9 - 3:02

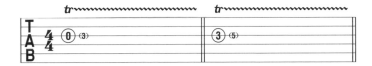

Trills can be used as a pretty texture. Below, they're played over an E major chord:

 ARTICULATIONS 10 - 3:40

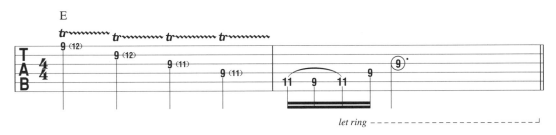

Here's an example that uses an open string:

 ARTICULATIONS 11 - 3:55

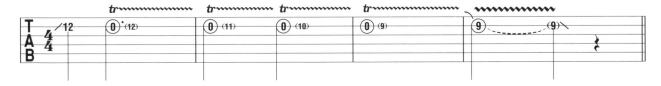

Trills can really add flavor to your lead playing.

FINGERINGS

I want to point out one thing I didn't talk about before, which is that, when you're performing your hammer-ons and pull-offs, there's no real rule in regard to which finger you use. Depending on where you're located on the neck, you may want to use your index and middle finger, your index and ring finger, or your index and pinky finger:

 ARTICULATIONS 12 - 4:26

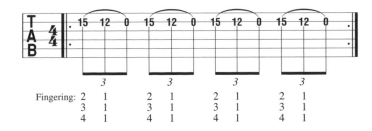

When I have a wider distance to reach—for example, when outlining chords on a single string—I tend to use my pinky. Here's a pull-off example outlining a B major chord with the index and pinky fingers:

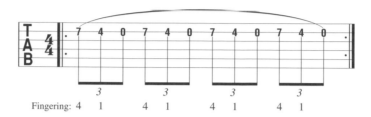

ARTICULATIONS 13 - 4:46

It's a matter of finding out what you're comfortable with.

SHAPE SHIFTING

I want to show you something really cool that involves shifting a hammer-on or pull-off shape, or pattern, up and down the neck.

ARTICULATIONS 14 - 5:02

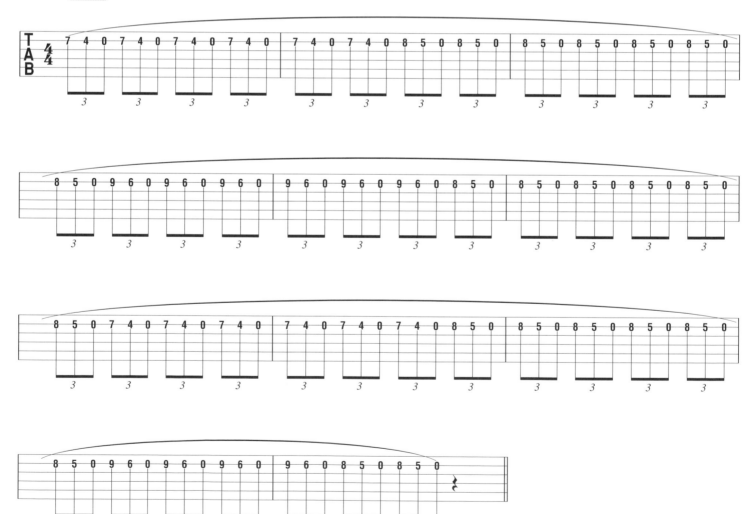

You can do that type of thing exclusively with hammer-ons, too:

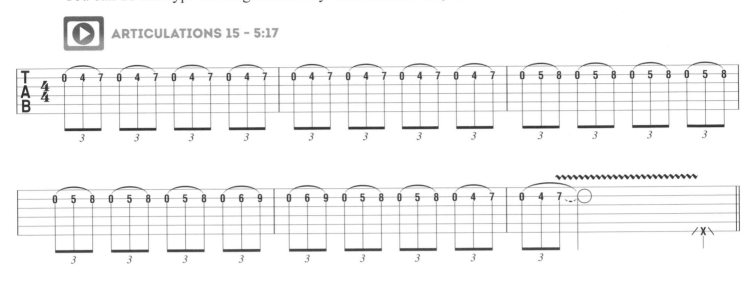

Let's look at another cool trick. Randy Rhoads did stuff like this a lot. It's based on the shifting pull-off pattern that we just discussed. Here's the premise: what if we moved the nut along with the shape? Basically, you place your pick hand over your fret hand and slide up the neck along with the pull-off pattern:

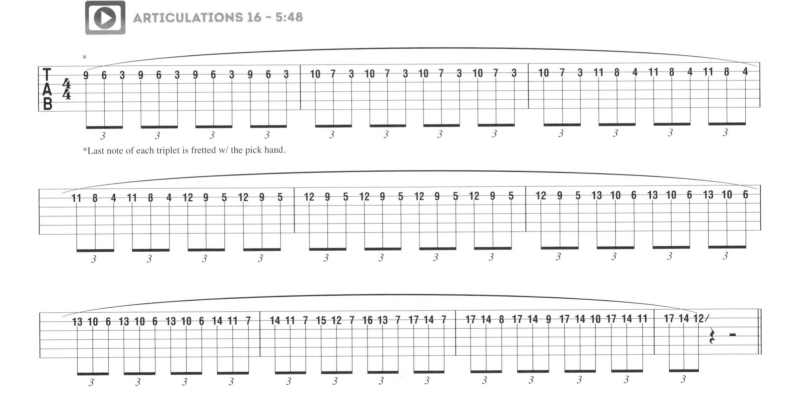

It's kind of a crazy effect, but it's *really* neat sometimes. You can also use it to bend:

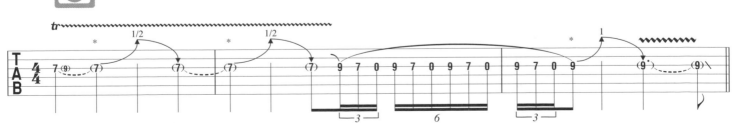

CHAPTER 7
HARMONICS

 **HARMONICS 1 - 0:00**

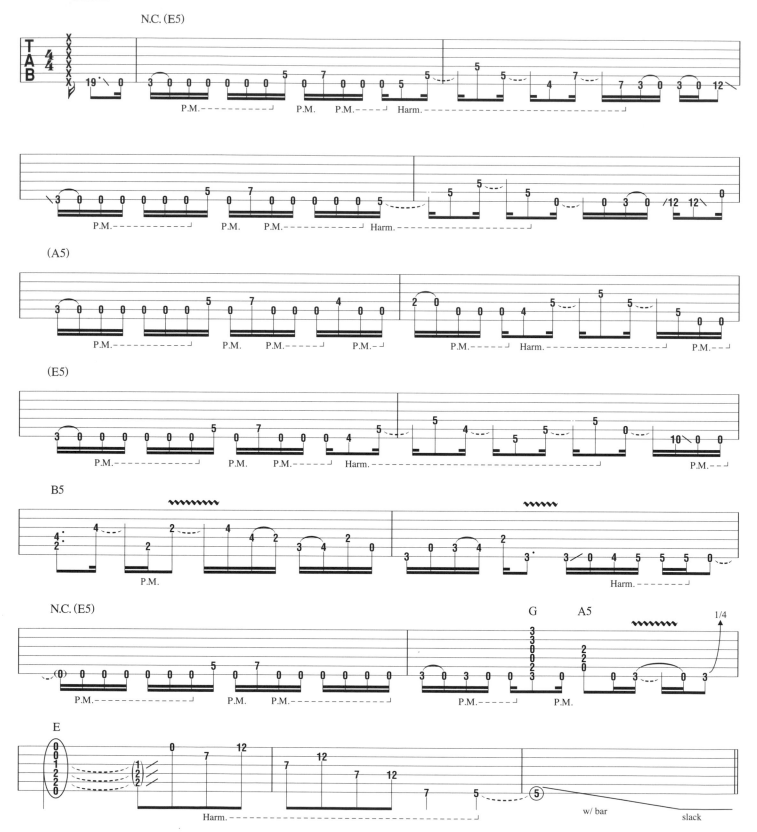

In this chapter, we're going to look at *harmonics*—specifically, the types that are used most commonly in rock 'n' roll. I'm going to walk you through them and show you how to play them yourself.

NATURAL HARMONICS

First, we'll look at open, or natural, harmonics. Generally, natural harmonics will be more pronounced at the 12th, seventh, and fifth frets. But, if you're using an overdriven rock sound, you'll be able to produce them just about anywhere, because that type of tone tends to enhance the harmonics.

 HARMONICS 2 - 1:05

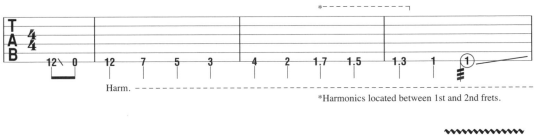

*Harmonics located between 1st and 2nd frets.

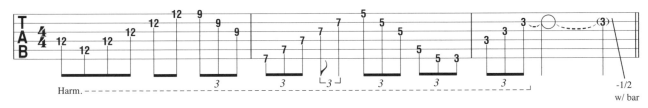

They're pretty much everywhere—all across the neck:

 **HARMONICS 3 - 1:21**

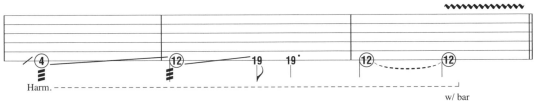

Natural harmonics are effective with both a clean sound and a dirty sound.

Producing these open-string harmonics is a matter of placing your finger across the fret wire, whether it's for a single note or multiple notes:

 **HARMONICS 4 - 1:45**

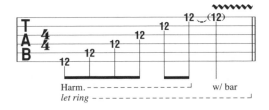

As opposed to pressing down and voicing the string, what you're really doing is laying your finger right above the fret wire, lightly touching the string, and then striking it with the pick. Once you've struck the note, you want to go ahead and lift your finger from the string. Generally, the harmonic will ring to some degree with your finger left in place, but you run the risk of losing the note, as it tends to drop off more quickly. So, if you want it to ring out, try to get your fingers away from the strings:

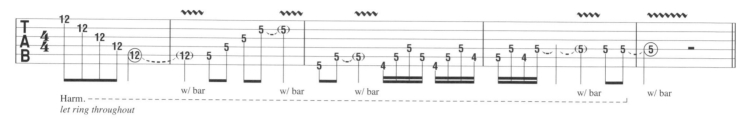

Once you get comfortable with this concept, you can start to find other places where harmonics are a little harder to achieve:

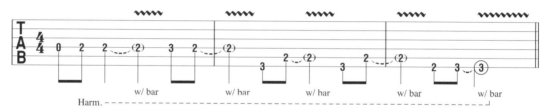

Eventually, you'll develop a touch and know exactly when to lift your finger from the string to get the tone to ring out:

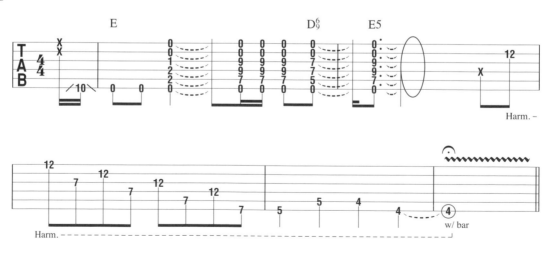

PINCH HARMONICS

 HARMONICS 8 - 3:22

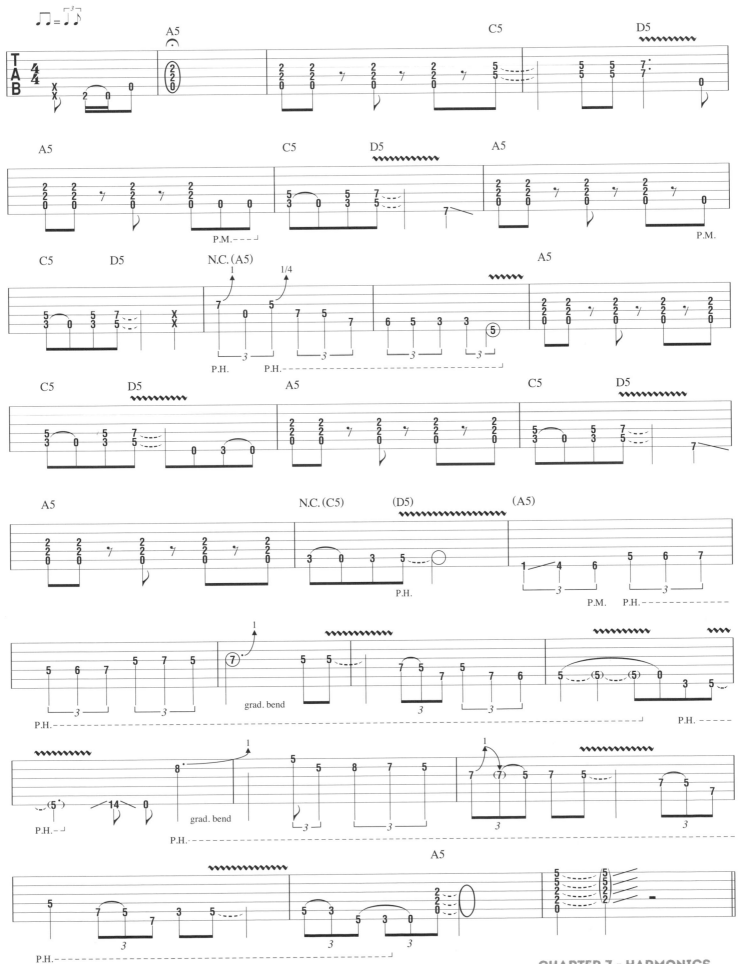

I also use a lot of pinch, or overtone, harmonics (indicated by "P.H." in the tab). ZZ Top's Billy Gibbons likes to use pinch harmonics often, as well—and so do many other players—but he does it in a particularly cool fashion:

 HARMONICS 9 - 4:16

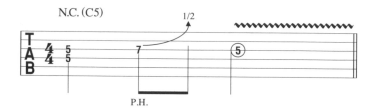

What makes Gibbons' pinch harmonics so special is the way he gets multiple tones from the same pitch by moving up and down the string with his pick:

 HARMONICS 10 - 4:25

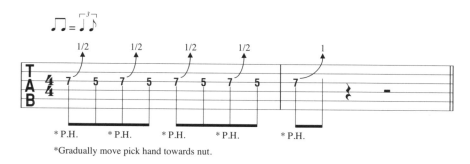

To execute pinch harmonics, fret and hold a note, striking the string with a downstroke like you would any other note while playing lead. The difference, however, is that you want to choke up on your guitar pick so that your thumb is at the very edge of it. That way, when you come across the string, your thumb is going to catch the edge of the string, changing it from a regular note to a harmonic. It's a bit of a tricky concept, but if you take it slowly and make sure your thumb is catching the string as you pick, you'll get it.

Pinch harmonics also work with lower notes, and you'll hear this from a lot of guitar players today:

 HARMONICS 11 - 6:28

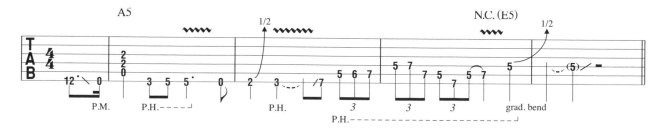

CHAPTER 8
TAPPING

 **TAPPING 1 - 0:00**

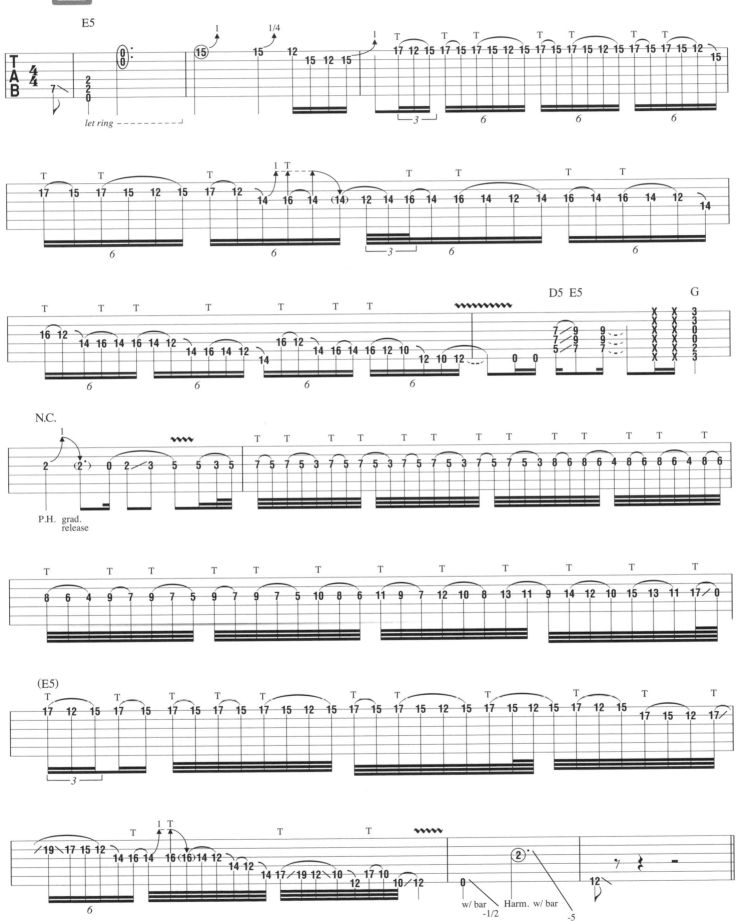

In this chapter, I want to talk to you about a fun technique called *tapping*, which is really just a matter of adding another set of fingers to the fretboard (pick hand and fret hand together). When you're playing leads, you can start to drop in a few notes:

TAPPING 2 - 0:57

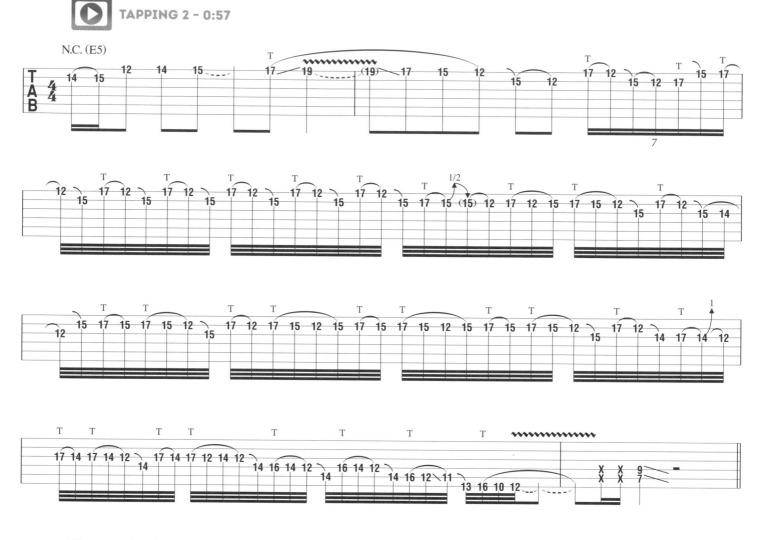

You can simulate super-fast runs or just use tapping to produce a nice triplet effect, which is something Eddie Van Halen did a lot:

TAPPING 3 - 1:21

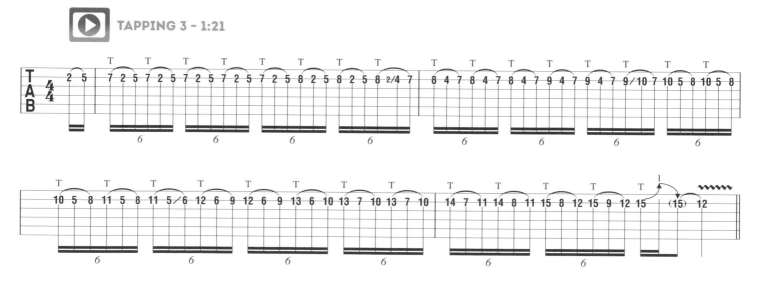

Eddie generally used these types of triplets on one string, and I use it from time to time, mostly as an effect. It's a really cool technique that you should try to learn.

WHERE TO PUT THE PICK?

Since you'll need a free finger on your tapping hand, you'll have to do something with your pick. What I like to do is stick it inside my hand, behind my middle finger, thereby freeing up my index finger to tap. When you need your pick, you can just pop it right back out and you're back in business!

TAPPING BASICS

Now, I want to go over a few tapping techniques. In case you're not far enough along to understand the concepts, I'm going to start really simply.

To start a triplet pattern, I'm using the index finger of my pick hand to pluck the first note (the pattern has to start somewhere!). However, you don't want to voice this note—you're just picking it. So, I'm starting with the pluck, hammering up from fret 3 to fret 5, and then tapping onto fret 7 with my pick-hand index finger. Once the sequence is complete, the pick-hand index finger then pulls off (plucks) the string to repeat the process.

TAPPING 4 - 3:57

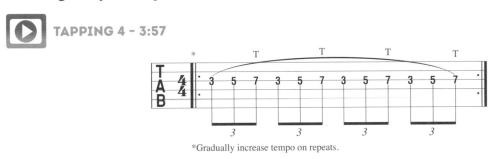

*Gradually increase tempo on repeats.

Work at that slowly and easily—you don't have to go fast. The key is to make each note sound balanced, smooth, and even.

Now let's move on to something with a few more notes. In the previous example, we ascended the G string with triplets. Now we're going to turn that around. This time, we're going to ignore the first rule—we *are* going to tap the first (highest) note in the pattern—and then pull off to the second and third notes:

TAPPING 5 - 4:33

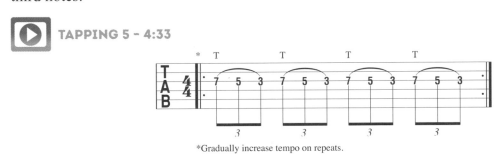

*Gradually increase tempo on repeats.

Again, you want the notes to be balanced. Here's one that both descends *and* ascends the pattern:

TAPPING 6 - 4:53

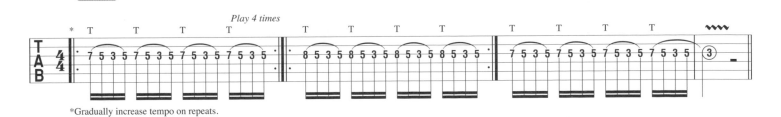

*Gradually increase tempo on repeats.

Now let's introduce another note to the same pattern. All we're going to do is remove the index finger in order to sound the open G string:

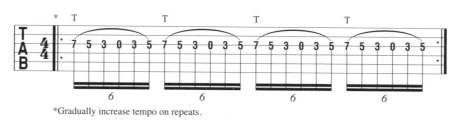

All the notes should sound pretty even, which is very important. Otherwise, the pattern will lose its fluidity. Now here's an example that incorporates the open string while both descending and ascending the pattern:

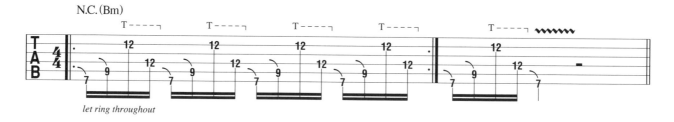

*Gradually increase tempo on repeats.

LEFT- AND RIGHT-HAND TAPPING

Our next technique involves a left-hand hammer. You may have seen other people do this; it's become quite popular today and is all over YouTube. Here's an example:

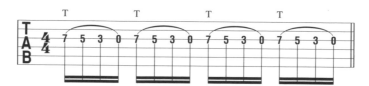

I use my pinky for this, but you can also use your ring finger. The fret-hand pattern is like a walk as it moves from the B note on the low E string to the F♯ on the A string. Meanwhile, your tapping hand plays another walking pattern. Tap your middle finger onto the 12th fret of the B string and your index finger onto the 12th fret of the D string. When you put both hands together, you get this nice, rolling, four-string pattern.

Once you have that down, you can start moving the pattern around:

 **TAPPING 10 - 7:36**

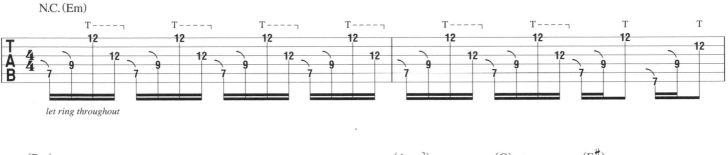

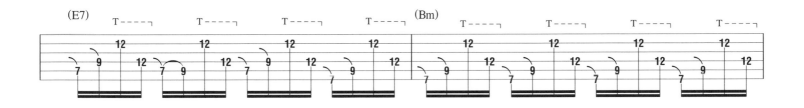

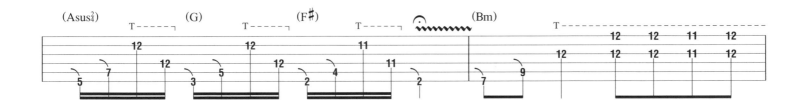

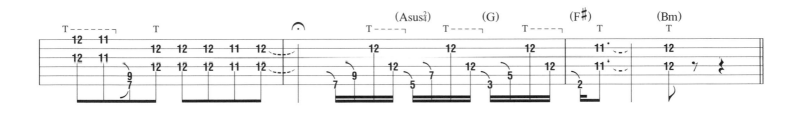

CHAPTER 9
DOUBLE STOPS

 DOUBLE STOPS 1 - 0:00

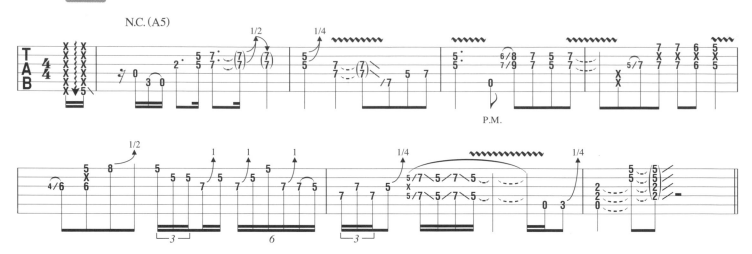

In this chapter, we'll look at another cool concept—*double stops*. Basically, we're taking two notes and using them together in an interesting way, whether it's bending, sliding, shaking the strings, etc. I have a couple of examples for you. We're going to take them one at time and then talk about what we're doing with each.

UNISON BENDS

 DOUBLE STOPS 2 - 0:43

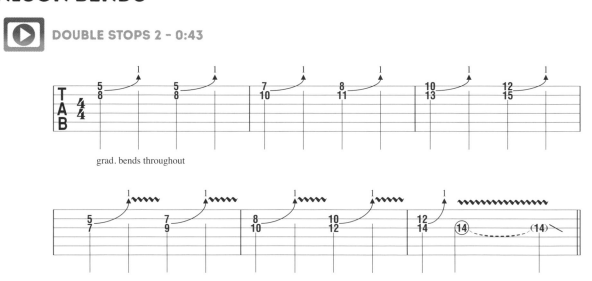

The example above involves playing a note (in the case of the first note, A) on the high E string with the index finger and bending a note on the B string with the ring finger. Unlike a typical bend-to-pitch type of thing, I deliberately want both notes to ring out at the same volume. You can also shake the bent note to give the double stop some nice tension. At times, it's almost better not to bend the note to perfect pitch; instead, leaving it a little flat, or going a little sharp, or shaking them to get that "rattle" (or modulation) between the two notes. The example starts on the B and high E strings, but, as you can see, unison bends work well on the G and B strings, too. In fact, one of the added benefits of playing them on the G and B strings is that you can let the high E string ring out underneath those strings.

Here's an example in the E minor pentatonic position:

 DOUBLE STOPS 3 - 2:35

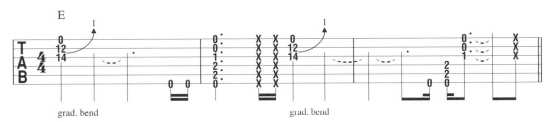

It's a very cool effect!

MINOR 3RD/MAJOR 3RD RUB

 DOUBLE STOPS 4 - 2:45

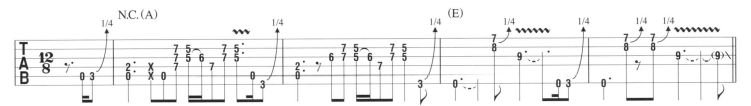

Now let's talk about a couple of more ideas while staying on the theme of double stops. The example above is a pentatonic-based blues progression that starts in the key of A. However, instead of strumming or arpeggiating the A major shape, I'm hammering from the minor 3rd (C) to the major 3rd (C♯). You want those two notes working in conjunction. By adding the E note on the B string (fret 5), you get a double stop. I'm also moving my ring finger in and out (fret 7) to give the figure some sass. Then, at measure 3, I move up to the E chord. This is a classic blues move, but it sounds great in heavy rock stuff, too. Gary Moore used it all the time.

6THS

Here's another idea. It starts at the ninth fret and moves down the neck in half steps. I'm using my middle and ring fingers on the G and E strings, respectively, skipping the B string:

 DOUBLE STOPS 5 - 5:43

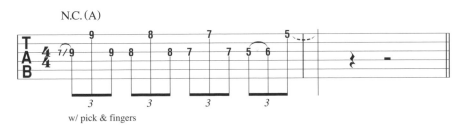

You can play it with straight double stops, but it sounds great when you separate the notes and play them as triplets (as shown). You can even shake the notes to give the phrase some attitude!

Here's the same idea, played on the D and B strings:

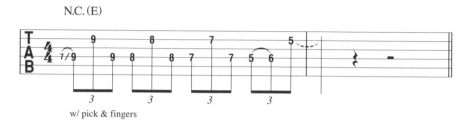

SLIDING DOUBLE STOPS

Lastly, I want to look at *sliding* double stops, something Jimi Hendrix did a lot.

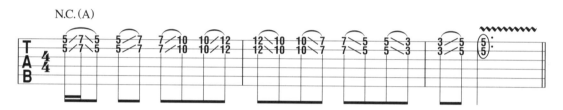

You can find sliding double stops all over the neck:

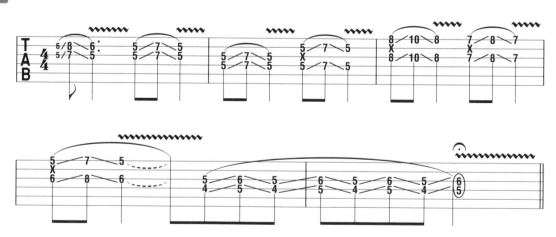

You can hear the blues connotation in there. Experiment with sliding double stops—they're everywhere and they're really effective!

CHAPTER 10
WARM-UPS AND CONDITIONING

This topic, warm-ups and conditioning, is really important. As you get into playing lead guitar, you're using individual fingers on your strings more so than when playing rhythm. Hand strength is a little more important at this point. You need to take care of the muscles and joints—all the things that work in tandem—to keep your fingers healthy. I used to be very religious about this, but now I use it when my hands feel a little stiff or if I'm in a cold-weather setting. That said, it's a really good practice to get into.

HAND MASSAGE AND STRETCHING

I start with a gentle massage around the whole hand, using my thumb for the areas outside of the palm and at the bottom of the thumb, where the biggest and strongest muscles are located. Those are the hardest to work through. This helps to loosen up, but it also helps to get blood into the extremities. Work it all the way down to your fingertips and make sure to do both hands, but particularly your fretting hand. There's nothing worse than blazing through some guitar licks with stiff, cold hands. You can probably get away with it when you're younger, but when you're older, you start to feel some of that stiffness.

Next, work from your wrist all the way up to your elbow. You can feel the ligaments and muscles under the skin, and you can tell when they're tight by moving your hands around. So do that to both arms. You'll be able to feel when you're starting to loosen up.

Once you feel loose, move to the index finger of your fret hand. Straighten your arm and gently pull back on the finger. Be careful—you don't want to just yank on it. That's a mistake, and you can really hurt yourself by doing that. You'll feel the tension right away in your arm and wrist. Hold the position for a little bit. Once you feel that tension, go ahead and move your free fingers the best you can. Do this with all of your fingers. If you do this every day, or three to four times a week, you'll notice that the travel in your fingers will increase; you'll be able to pull them back farther. If you feel any pain or discomfort while doing this, put less pressure on the finger as you pull it back. Don't overdo it; you'll get there in time.

Due to the size of the muscles, you'll approach the thumb and pinky differently. You want to pull the pinky towards your body (at an inward angle) rather than straight back. That's the only way to get the proper extension. Do the same thing with the thumb, only pulling it in the opposite direction. Remember: you're trying to stretch, not prove how far you can stretch your fingers.

The next stretch is basically the opposite of what we just did. Now you're going to gently pull your thumb downward and toward your body and wiggle your free fingers. This will help stretch a different set of muscles. Start with the thumb and then move on down the line.

A lot of things you do when playing lead guitar involve pretty wide stretches, and they can be really uncomfortable, at least in the beginning. To help with this, I'd like to share with you a couple of stretches. You can use them at your leisure. I would encourage you to do them very gently and carefully at first. As your reach starts to widen and your hands become stronger, you can be a little more liberal with them. But, again, start gently.

Everyone wants to use crazy-wide stretches when playing lead guitar, and it's certainly a handy technique, so what I did—and this is sort of unconventional—is take two fingers (index and middle, middle and ring, etc.) and, while watching TV or doing some other leisurely activity, place them on the back of my guitar's neck, around the fretboard. Every guitar is different—some are wider and some are narrower—so you need to be careful. Your guide should be how your fingers feel. After you ease your fingers onto the neck, just let them sit there for 30–45 seconds. Don't ram them all the way forward. If you do, you're going to tear something. If you feel any pain or discomfort, back away and narrow your stretch. In as soon as a couple of weeks, you'll get to a point where you're all the way up to the back of the neck. Over time, your muscles will get used to opening up like that, which will help widen your reach. Again, do not force anything, as it will create a setback for you.

The last stretch I want to show you involves putting both of your hands straight out in front of your body, palms down, and using their own strength to stretch the fingers as far and wide as they go. Do this for 15–20 seconds and then relax them. You should feel some heat on both forearms. Do this a few times. It will help maintain flexibility and mobility in both hands and, most importantly, keep them healthy.

EXERCISE

Now let's move on to an exercise that involves actual playing and will help with dexterity and coordination. It's not particularly musical, but it's great for your hands. I used it constantly on tour because it didn't matter if there was noise around me; it's actually more about the feel of it than the sound. What you're going to do is play four notes on each string, like this:

▶ WARM-UPS 1 - 10:32

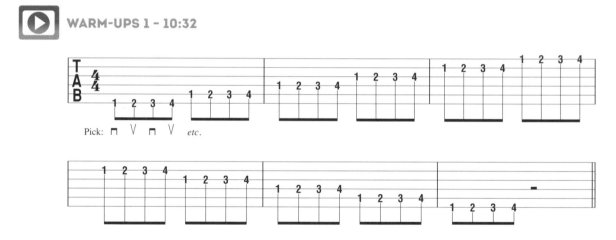

Be sure to use alternate picking. I realize the exercise might sound mundane, but that's not really the point. The aim is to get your fingers rolling and to work on your right- and left-hand coordination.

Here's the same exercise in reverse:

▶ WARM-UPS 2 - 10:50

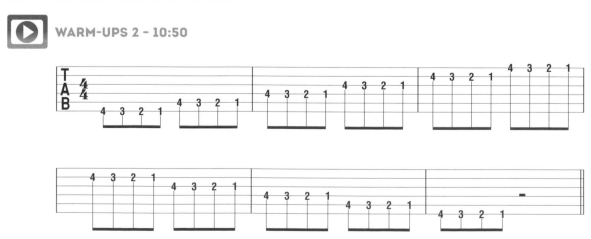

CHAPTER 11
REPEATING LICKS

In this chapter, we'll look at repeating licks, which I use a lot. Repeating licks are great when you're trying to create tension. If a lick sounds great once, it's probably going to sound great a bunch of times, especially really fast. Let me give you some examples…

 REPEATING LICKS 1 - 0:15

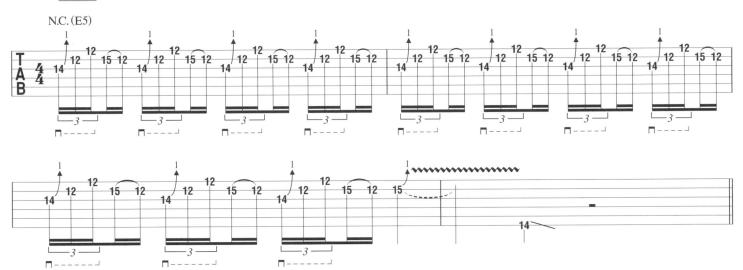

In that lick, I started with my ring finger for the whole-step G-string bend, followed by a sweep through the bend and the short barre across the B and E strings at fret 12. For the pull-off, you can use either your pinky or your ring finger. I use my pinky and pull off to my index finger, which is now fretting the B string at the 12th fret.

Here's another repeating lick:

 **REPEATING LICKS 2 - 2:10**

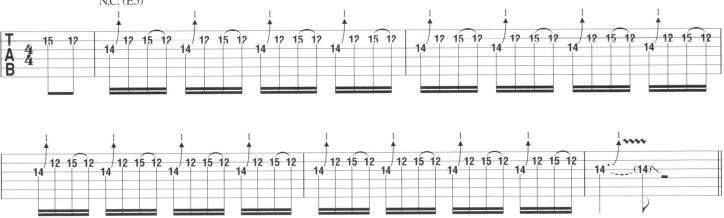

Similar to the first lick, this one stays away from the high E string. I'm working exclusively between the G and B strings. I start with ring and index fingers on the 15th and 12th frets of the B string, respectively, and use my middle finger for the G-string bend. When you play this slowly and kind of break up the notes, it sounds like a Paul Kossoff (guitarist for the band Free) or Jimmy Page thing. As you get faster and faster, it moves into Gary Moore territory.

Here's a variation of the previous lick. This one sounds a little more menacing. Instead of using your middle finger for the 14th fret of the G string, slide it up to the 15th fret.

REPEATING LICKS 3 - 3:28

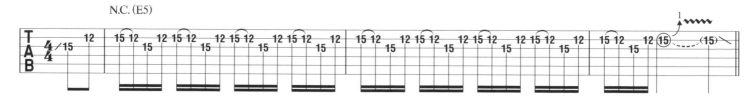

Here's another one:

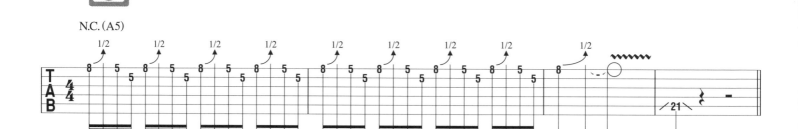

REPEATING LICKS 4 - 3:34

That's a Jimi Hendrix-style lick. When I'm grabbing the strings for these types of bends while trying to play fast licks, I'm not bending with just one finger—that would be extremely difficult. Instead, I'm using the strength of all three fingers: index, middle, and ring. The faster you play this lick, the cooler it sounds!

Here's the last repeating lick that I want to show you:

REPEATING LICKS 5 - 4:35

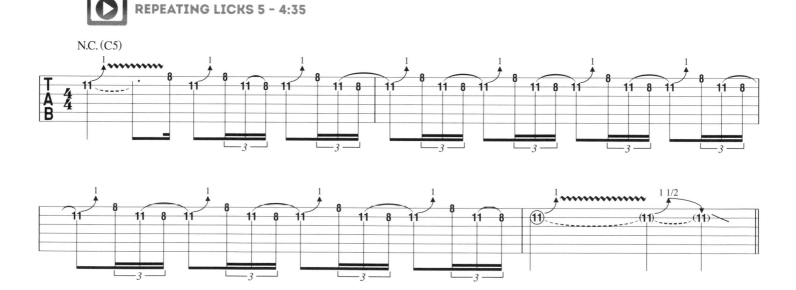

This is a fast lick that's played in the C minor pentatonic position. Basically, I'm starting with a ring-finger bend of the B string. There are only three notes involved: B♭ (string 2, fret 11), C (string 1, fret 8), and G (string 2, fret 8). Played slowly, I'm double picking the B string. As it gets faster, it sounds cooler to omit one of the pick attacks, settling for a single downstroke on the B string and single upstroke on the high E string. What I'm doing is pulling, hammering, and bending the three B-string notes.

CHAPTER 12
GETTING GREAT LEAD TONE AND USING EFFECTS

▶ TONE AND EFFECTS 1 - 0:00

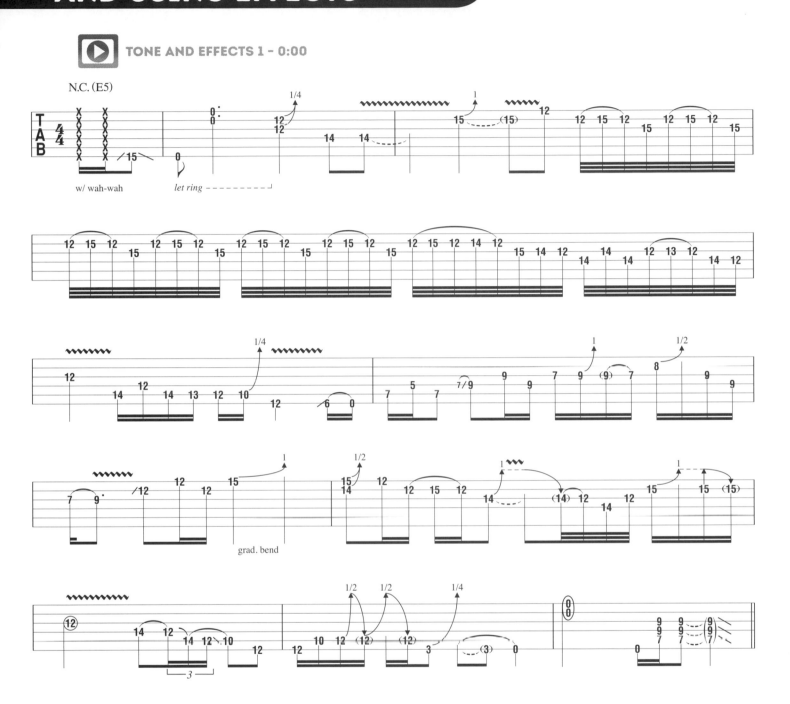

GUITAR AND AMP

In this chapter, I want to talk to you about *tone*. Great lead tones start with a great guitar and a great tube amp. A tube amp and a Gibson Les Paul or Fender Stratocaster have always been my weapons of choice. But what you decide is entirely up to you.

At the core of great tone is a great-playing, good-sounding, reliable instrument. As I mentioned, I like Les Pauls and Strats, but they can't be just any old guitar; they really need to be set up to play well. The neck needs to be adjusted properly. It's great to have a decent fret dress so your frets are even in height and your notes ring out well. Your guitar should be intonated properly, and you should have good, functioning electronics. Also, your tuners should work properly so you can keep the guitar in tune.

Additionally, you should have a great-sounding tube amp that you can use at high or low gain and it will give you a myriad of sounds:

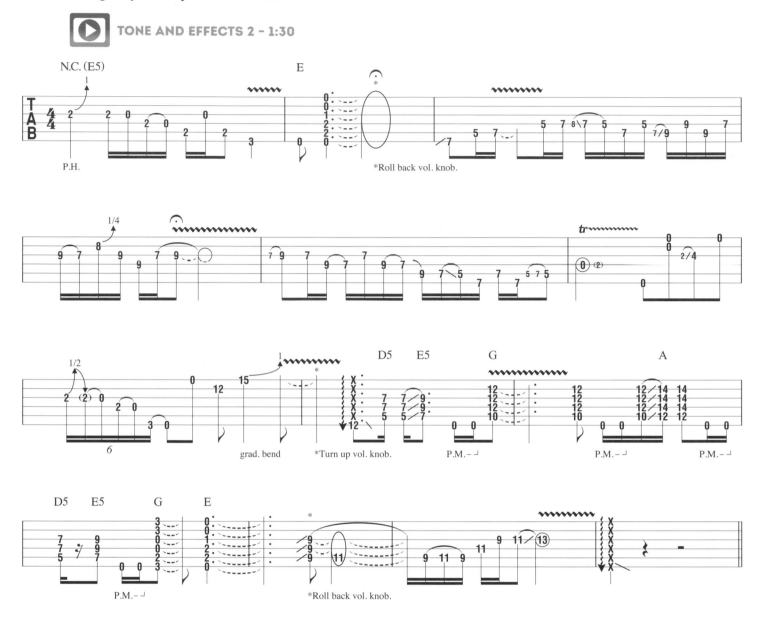

TONE AND EFFECTS 2 - 1:30

A good amp will clean up with the volume rolled back. If you have an amp that gives you a little bit of everything, you're on your way.

PICKUPS

Along with having a good, solid-playing guitar and a great-sounding amp, I like to have a certain kind of pickup in the guitar. If it's a humbucking pickup, I don't like it to be a high-output pickup. In my opinion, a medium-to-low output pickup sounds better because it allows the sound of the guitar to come through the amplifier more. Otherwise, you're just listening to the amp. When you roll the volume back, your guitar should come through.

EFFECTS

Now, let's talk about effects. With the core being a great-sounding amp and a great-sounding guitar, it's nice to have a little bit of frosting on top. Effects that I use include fuzz, compressor, wah, delay, chorus, and phaser. There are all kinds of different modulation pedals, as well.

I want to discuss a couple of ideas to help you with your sound. First, it's great to have some type of boost. Sometimes I use fuzz, but many effects will work, including a compressor or wah pedal. Those two effects are great when you want the following types of lines to really sing:

 TONE AND EFFECTS 3 - 3:43

The boost is very subtle. Here's another one:

 TONE AND EFFECTS 4 - 3:59

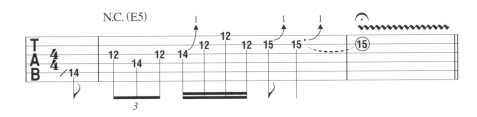

Again, when you're adding gain, boost, or distortion to your sound, you don't want it to be so over the top that the tone is out of control and you end up losing the guitar. You just want it to push your sound forward, enhance it, and give it a little extra sustain.

As mentioned above, you could also use a wah pedal to achieve the desired boost. By moving it into different positions, not only is it a tone control…

 TONE AND EFFECTS 5 - 4:37

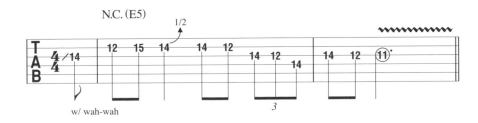

…but it will drive your tone straight through. Michael Schenker was great at finding that sweet spot.

Here's another example:

TONE AND EFFECTS 6 - 4:49

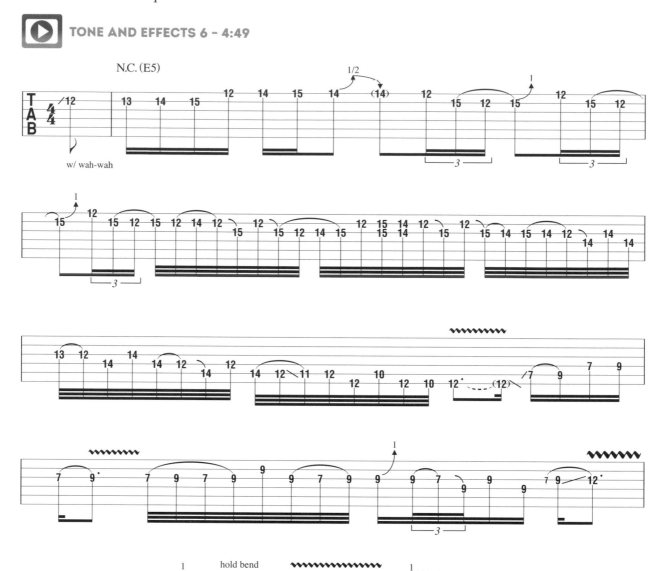

Of course, you could also use it as a traditional wah pedal:

TONE AND EFFECTS 7 - 5:12

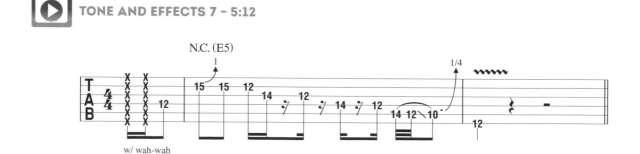

Another thing that I like to add to some of my leads, especially if I'm looking for a little space or something kind of pretty, is a bit of delay:

 TONE AND EFFECTS 8 - 5:45

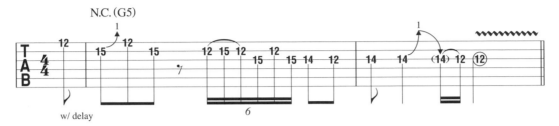

As you set up your delays and start to use them in your songs, you'll begin to figure out what works. For rhythm playing, you probably don't want to get into a whole bunch of long delays. But for lead work, you can get away with longer delays that sound pretty cool:

 TONE AND EFFECTS 9 - 6:03

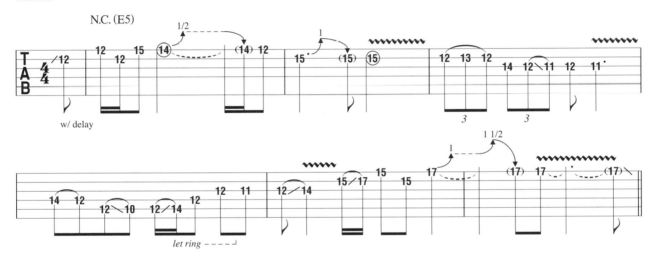

CLOSING JAM

In closing, I'd like to offer a few suggestions to help you develop your playing:

1. Practice your scales and lead playing with a drum machine, looper, or metronome. While not quite as inspirational as drums, metronomes will help improve your timing.

2. Listen to other guitar players. Listen to their tones, phrasing, vibrato, and overall feel of what they're doing. Notice where they leave space for other instruments, especially vocals.

3. Try to incorporate vibrato, space, and feel into your own playing to make it more emotional. That's what *really* connects with the listener.

Great soloing makes for great-feeling music. Good luck and keep on jammin'!

▶ CLOSING JAM - 0:38

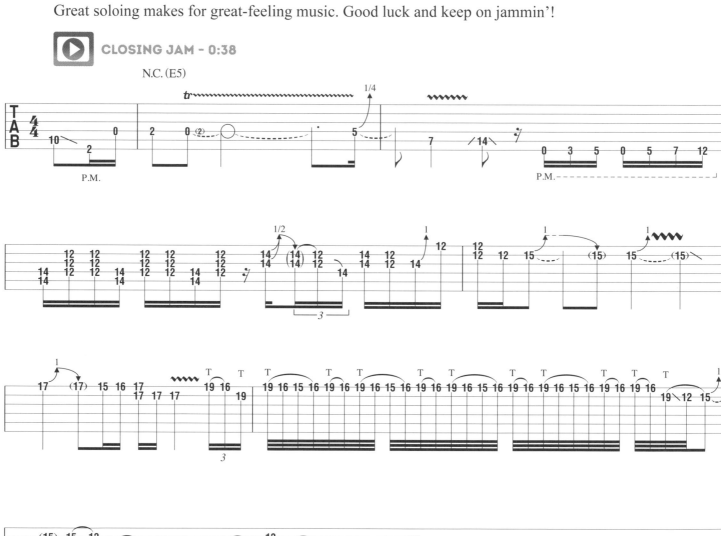

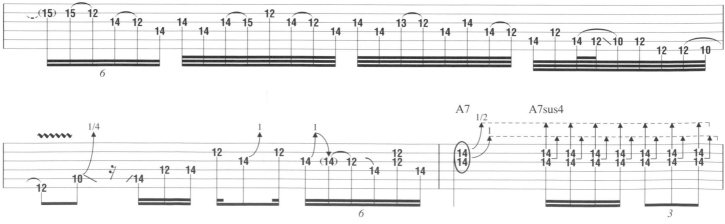

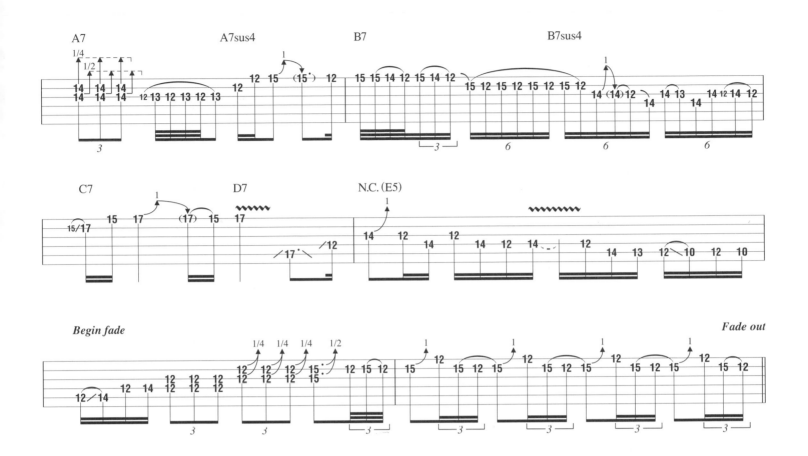

Get Better at Guitar

...with these Great Guitar Instruction Books from Hal Leonard!

101 GUITAR TIPS
INCLUDES TAB

STUFF ALL THE PROS KNOW AND USE

by Adam St. James

This book contains invaluable guidance on everything from scales and music theory to truss rod adjustments, proper recording studio set-ups, and much more. The book also features snippets of advice from some of the most celebrated guitarists and producers in the music business, including B.B. King, Steve Vai, Joe Satriani, Warren Haynes, Laurence Juber, Pete Anderson, Tom Dowd and others, culled from the author's hundreds of interviews.

00695737 Book/Online Audio $16.99

AMAZING PHRASING
INCLUDES TAB

50 WAYS TO IMPROVE YOUR IMPROVISATIONAL SKILLS

by Tom Kolb

This book/CD pack explores all the main components necessary for crafting well-balanced rhythmic and melodic phrases. It also explains how these phrases are put together to form cohesive solos. Many styles are covered – rock, blues, jazz, fusion, country, Latin, funk and more – and all of the concepts are backed up with musical examples. The companion CD contains 89 demos for listening, and most tracks feature full-band backing.

00695583 Book/CD Pack...$19.95

BLUES YOU CAN USE – 2ND EDITION

by John Ganapes

This comprehensive source for learning blues guitar is designed to develop both your lead and rhythm playing. Includes: 21 complete solos • blues chords, progressions and riffs • turnarounds • movable scales and soloing techniques • string bending • utilizing the entire fingerboard • and more. This second edition now includes audio and video access online!

00142420 Book/Online Media.................................$19.99

FRETBOARD MASTERY
INCLUDES TAB

by Troy Stetina

Untangle the mysterious regions of the guitar fretboard and unlock your potential. *Fretboard Mastery* familiarizes you with all the shapes you need to know by applying them in real musical examples, thereby reinforcing and reaffirming your newfound knowledge. The result is a much higher level of comprehension and retention.

00695331 Book/Online Audio $19.99

FRETBOARD ROADMAPS – 2ND EDITION

ESSENTIAL GUITAR PATTERNS THAT ALL THE PROS KNOW AND USE

by Fred Sokolow

The updated edition of this bestseller features more songs, updated lessons, and a full audio CD! Learn to play lead and rhythm anywhere on the fretboard, in any key; play a variety of lead guitar styles; play chords and progressions anywhere on the fretboard; expand your chord vocabulary; and learn to think musically – the way the pros do.

00695941 Book/CD Pack..$14.95

GUITAR AEROBICS
INCLUDES TAB

A 52-WEEK, ONE-LICK-PER-DAY WORKOUT PROGRAM FOR DEVELOPING, IMPROVING & MAINTAINING GUITAR TECHNIQUE

by Troy Nelson

From the former editor of *Guitar One* magazine, here is a daily dose of vitamins to keep your chops fine tuned! Musical styles include rock, blues, jazz, metal, country, and funk. Techniques taught include alternate picking, arpeggios, sweep picking, string skipping, legato, string bending, and rhythm guitar. These exercises will increase speed, and improve dexterity and pick- and fret-hand accuracy. The accompanying audio includes all 365 workout licks plus play-along grooves in every style at eight different metronome settings.

00695946 Book/Online Audio $19.99

GUITAR CLUES
INCLUDES TAB

OPERATION PENTATONIC

by Greg Koch

Join renowned guitar master Greg Koch as he clues you in to a wide variety of fun and valuable pentatonic scale applications. Whether you're new to improvising or have been doing it for a while, this book/CD pack will provide loads of delicious licks and tricks that you can use right away, from volume swells and chicken pickin' to intervallic and chordal ideas. The CD includes 65 demo and play-along tracks.

00695827 Book/CD Pack...$19.95

INTRODUCTION TO GUITAR TONE & EFFECTS

by David M. Brewster

This book/CD pack teaches the basics of guitar tones and effects, with audio examples on CD. Readers will learn about: overdrive, distortion and fuzz • using equalizers • modulation effects • reverb and delay • multi-effect processors • and more.

00695766 Book/CD Pack..$14.99

PICTURE CHORD ENCYCLOPEDIA

This comprehensive guitar chord resource for all playing styles and levels features five voicings of 44 chord qualities for all twelve keys – 2,640 chords in all! For each, there is a clearly illustrated chord frame, as well as *an actual photo* of the chord being played! Includes info on basic fingering principles, open chords and barre chords, partial chords and broken-set forms, and more.

00695224..$19.95

SCALE CHORD RELATIONSHIPS
INCLUDES TAB

by Michael Mueller & Jeff Schroedl

This book teaches players how to determine which scales to play with which chords, so guitarists will never have to fear chord changes again! This book/audio pack explains how to: recognize keys • analyze chord progressions • use the modes • play over nondiatonic harmony • use harmonic and melodic minor scales • use symmetrical scales such as chromatic, whole-tone and diminished scales • incorporate exotic scales such as Hungarian major and Gypsy minor • and much more!

00695563 Book/Online Audio $14.99

SPEED MECHANICS FOR LEAD GUITAR
INCLUDES TAB

Take your playing to the stratosphere with the most advanced lead book by this proven heavy metal author. *Speed Mechanics* is the ultimate technique book for developing the kind of speed and precision in today's explosive playing styles. Learn the fastest ways to achieve speed and control, secrets to make your practice time really count, and how to open your ears and make your musical ideas more solid and tangible. Packed with over 200 vicious exercises including Troy's scorching version of "Flight of the Bumblebee." Music and examples demonstrated on CD. 89-minute audio.

00699323 Book/CD Pack...$19.95

TOTAL ROCK GUITAR
INCLUDES TAB

A COMPLETE GUIDE TO LEARNING ROCK GUITAR

by Troy Stetina

This unique and comprehensive source for learning rock guitar is designed to develop both lead and rhythm playing. It covers: getting a tone that rocks • open chords, power chords and barre chords • riffs, scales and licks • string bending, strumming, palm muting, harmonics and alternate picking • all rock styles • and much more. The examples are in standard notation with chord grids and tab, and the audio includes full-band backing for all 22 songs.

00695246 Book/Online Audio $19.99

HAL•LEONARD® CORPORATION

7777 W. BLUEMOUND RD. P.O. BOX 13819 MILWAUKEE, WI 53213

Visit Hal Leonard Online at
www.halleonard.com

Prices, contents, and availability subject to change without notice.

0616